In Praise of Japanese Love Poems

In Praise of Japanese Love Poems

Introduction by Regina Sara Ryan
Poems by Lee Lozowick et al.

HOHM PRESS · PRESCOTT, ARIZONA

INTRODUCTION

How desperately we toughened, analytical thinkers of the computer age need the reminder of the solitary plum branch against the grey sky. As the gap between ourselves and nature widens, we suffer—personally and culturally. If, however, we can allow ourselves a free moment in which to observe the movement of one sparrow, to enjoy the camaraderie of two yellow mums, to drop into the silence of a virgin snowfield, then we will have left the restricted domain of mind and entered into the body of experience. "And it is with this body," as the poet Robert Bly says, that we will "...love the earth."

The poems in this eclectic anthology, *In Praise of Japanese Love Poetry*, come from an assembly of contemporary poets with two things in common. First, each has faith in things other than logic, and second, each has found in the traditional Japanese *haiku* or *tonka* a form that works exquisitely to express his or her sentiments of desire, love, and suffering.

Like their predecessors, these poets dare to grant significance and relationship to the simultaneous occurrence of two previously unrelated events. Their sharpened eye and longing heart is able to turn a smooth stone into palpable flesh, or the nervous wings of a butterfly into the eyelids of a shy lover. Thus sacralizing all of existence, each event in creation becomes for them a means of prayer—a means of lifting the mind and heart to remembrance of the Beloved.

The beauty and the challenge of writing about love and the Beloved is that the secret truths which the body knows, particularly in its most ecstatic moments, have the tendency to slip away when shifted into language. To attempt to write a definitive treatise on love, then, is probably ultimate folly. To write three to five lines of poetry which insinuate a mood of tenderness or passion seems like a much wiser choice—one that the elegant Japanese have indeed mastered over the centuries.

The power in these poems is that they are not descriptions,

because descriptions never show us things as they really are. Rather, these love poems are infections of emotion—a few well-chosen words designed to call forth the inherent emotional power that lives in all things. Enough. The reader's imagination can supply the rest.

The lovers whose poems are represented here have used these short verses like rose-petals dropped on the stairs leading the way to the bed chamber. In actuality, many of the traditional Japanese love poems were composed as invitations to a romantic engagement. The recipient was left to judge from the delicacy of the lines and their rhythm, the texture of the paper on which they were written, the fineness of the calligraphy, and the sweet aroma of the attached blossom or twig, whether the suitor's plea was worthy of acceptance. A poem was then sent in response. After a night of lovemaking, and as a token of appreciation, the lovers might also exchange poems capturing one distinctive element of their blissful encounter. The failure to receive a "morning after" poem might also herald the decline of the affair, and cause great pain to either or both of the lovers.

Imagine, in our day of answering machine intimacy, the raw excitement of receiving a personal, hand delivered note, carefully printed on perfumed stationary. Who among us would not blush with anticipation upon opening the daily mail to find these lines:

> This January night
>   As the wings of my kimono open
> I stand before you, alone,
>   And shivering.

What an invitation! What a promise to carry like a warm secret throughout the long hours of the workday. And, with the meeting, what exhilaration with the first small hand gesture that commences the unfastening.

For the poet, as much as for the reader, these pieces enliven a mood of love. She, or he, must re-live the moment fully, or dream it so carefully, in order to capture it so succinctly. Thus, without leaving the writing desk the play of love begins, or continues. Dreams and memories given form have power!

These poets are courageous in the way that only lovers can be. Their caution is not thrown to the wind, however, but woven into a delicate verse. Like a single brushstroke, these terse poems are stark against the empty page, seducing the reader through a tiny door into a fresh-aired world, a world of first thoughts, a world not yet painted in the "united colors of benetton," sometimes a world of high intrigue and almost always a world in which simple truthtelling is the currency. The Buddhist worldview of emptiness and nowness explode, silently, in every piece.

Poetry flowers out of the stuff of our daily lives—the raw stuff, the insignificant stuff, the profound stuff. And the poems in this collection express sentiments from the humorous to the erotic, from the mundane to the esoteric. Three themes predominate here, however—loving, grieving, and waiting. These universal themes provide endless possibilities for commentary, because when people are in love everything speaks to them of the Beloved—

> The slender shoots
> Of new bamboo
> Oh, your ankles.
> and
> The fig tree is heavy
> With fruit
> Their musk
> Fills my senses

When people grieve, everything reminds them of the loss—

Leaves like pieces
Of a broken heart lie
At the feet of barren trees
You were gone before I knew you

or as one poet tenderly reminds us:

The sandal maker is eighty years old.
Each time I visit he points out the chair
Where his wife used to sit.
I nod, understanding.

And when people are waiting, each moment expands endlessly,
filled with either agony or ecstasy:

Waiting has its rewards
Today I watched
A purple hyacinth
Exploding.

or

Beneath this silk kimono
I am naked.
Why are you not here?

or more philosophically,

A cherry blossom
Always falls
At the right time.

It is unfortunate, perhaps, to publish a *collection* of such
intimate poems when each one deserves its own frame, its own
wall on which to hang, or its own piece of parchment and waxed

seal. Nevertheless, the cautioned reader can approach this poetry as one might wisely sample the delicacies on a banquet table—taking the time. Savoring.

Japanese poets, as others, often wrote poems paralleling, enhancing, or responding to the poems of the masters who inspired them. It is considered an acknowledgement to take the same elements used by a master and to compose a variation on a theme, in much the way that musicians, both classical and modern, will compose upon the style of another. Imitation is a form of tribute, and it is in this spirit of eminent regard and celebration that these humble poems are offered.

In presenting this small bouquet we have decided to group all the poems of one poet together, rather than interspersing them with those of others in a thematic or seasonal arrangement as is sometimes done. It is hoped that the uniqueness and the subtleties of each poet's moods can be more deeply appreciated in this way.

Another editorial decision which has veered somewhat from other more traditional collections is that these pieces are presented anonymously. Our thinking here is that the mood of love is easily shattered by the intrusion of the analytical mind which is fascinated and thus distracted by dates and names and places. When the heart is lifting, we would encourage it to soar.

In conclusion, it is hoped that this modest offering upon the altar of the great masters of Japanese love poetry may serve as inspiration to all who happen upon them. May our readers be moved to pick up their own pens, to remember the eyes of their Beloved, to inhale the fragrance of the wet grass, and to fly.

Regina Sara Ryan
February 1994

CALLIGRAPHY

Calligraphy by Denise Puck Wong

情詩

We didn't notice
      The fire had gone out
Until it was time for tea

                        My friends tell stories
                             Of many loves
                        I think only of you

            The ripe plum
                 Has no choice but to fall
            When its time comes
                 Did you think I would be different?

In the garden the plum tree's
    Branches spread wide
Where are you now?

                    My head upon the pillow
                        Feathers hard as rocks
                    Compared to you

        I sit by the brook
          Fishing idly
        Remembering last night

Your father and I
    Used to be friends
Before he awoke
    In the middle of the night

                The mountain is shrouded in mist
                    Like my eyes
                Since you left

    The spring rains
        Soak the eager earth
  Ah! my darling

Walls of rice paper
Leave nothing
To the imagination

> The hummingbird
> Visits my flowers
> Do you think of me?

> A praying mantis is not to be trusted
> With a grasshopper
> She is so young!

The scent of cherry blossoms
    In the spring breeze
Will I see you tonight?

                    Your old maid
                        Brought your answer
                    What will I do now?

            At the roadside inn
                The single poppy
            Reminds me of you

The slender shoots
    Of new bamboo
Oh, your ankles

           The way you blushed
               When I passed your window
           Be careful, my girl!

     When you lower
       Your eyes
     Mind open wide

The morning dew
    Reminds me too much
Of you

                To everyone else
                    The bellows fans the flames
                I alone think of you

        Wandering along the path
            Thinking of you
        I bumped into the willow tree

Even though the house is a mess
    My husband doesn't mind
He thinks it is him

          The wax slowly runs
              Down the side of the candle
          A sigh escapes

    The hot tea
        Has burned my lip
   Rather it were you

Oh mother
   It is the heavy load
That has marked my shoulders

                    Grandmother,
                        Catching my smile
                    Remembers long, long ago

      That cat,
         We must cut his claws
      See what he has done!

I love the moon
    When I'm with you
Because I never see it

                    No matter how many clouds
                        Moon rises
                    I remember your cheek

    How amazing!
        Just as the clock struck three,
    You and I.

10

The roof groans
    Under its load of snow
I think I will wake you again

        How tragic! The ripe persimmon
           Laying on the ground, uneaten.
        Won't you return soon?

We will plant in spring
   But for now
You have called me
   To your side

                How can I think of God
                    When you
              Are near?

        The rain sounds
           Like footsteps
       When will I see you again?

Leaves like pieces
  Of a broken heart lie
At the feet of barren trees
  You were gone before I knew you

Plum blossoms encased in ice
    By an unexpected frost
My heart since you left

                The sun softens
                    The frozen lake in spring
                Will you visit tonight?

        Snow falls
           And slowly fills the tracks
        Of your leaving

White crane bends gracefully
    To dip her wing in the water
Oh, my love!

Dropping my kimono
    Your eyelids pretend to be
Two shy butterflies

        Two yellow mums
           Anchored in smooth black stones
        Together we are delicate and unshaken

    Dancing shadows of a hundred
        Candle flames leap from my bed
    As you lay me down, gently

My bed is empty
    My heart is broken
Return. Return.

        The tea in your cup grows cold
           The coals in the brazier crumble
        And the yellow plums soften in their bowl
           Forgive me, my Lord
        I am blind to everything except the light
           That plays between your tongue and teeth

    This January night
        As the wings of my kimono open
    I stand before you, alone,
        And shivering

Stay away my Lord
    Until my fingernails grow sharp
With possibility

My instrument is not in
    Perfect tune
Yet you still want a love song!

          The raven soars
             In the cloudless sky
          My thoughts fly to you

      This garden is lush and ripe
        A perfect place
      To long for you

This bonsai has won me
    Such acclaim
And it merely occupied my time
    Away from you

This head has forgotten
　　How to move
Your shoulder casts spells

　　　　　　Get up! Get up!
　　　　　　　　What time is it?
　　　　　　Tell me who cares.

My other lovers satisfy
    But you leave me
Starving
    Why do I want only you?

                    An infant's foot
                        In delicate repose
                    Reminds me of you

        Ha! Cruel lover
            Thinks I care
        I'm just hungry!

A cherry blossom
Always falls
At the right time

                        Sitting in the
                            Bamboo grove
                        Snow falling
                            You breathing

        A long winter
            He cannot come
        Will I survive until spring?

The mountain snow
   Melts into waterfalls
The poems keep coming
   Where is my pen?

              The neighbors
                  Complained of cats
            Fighting late
              Into the night

      The moonlit night
         Is hiding
    Your eyes from me
       What a shame!

The cherry blossoms droop
  Like my breasts
When you're gone

                A winter day
                    Yields itself to spring
                For just a moment

    A silk kimono
        Of bright blue
    Reveals so much

Tatami mats
 And incense
Don't even come close
 Katsu!

26

Morning comes
    And you are gone
A slow rain falls

                Sunlight streams
                  Through red petals,
              Trembling, like my heart

      Petals lay fallen,
          Dry and wilted
    When will my lord return?

Ice melts, dripping slowly
    from dark branches—
How warm your hands!

                    The reeds grow green and tall
                        In still water
                    Here alone,
                        One white lily

Outside the wind howls
    Here, with my lord,
The snow melts

The fig tree is heavy
    With fruit
Their musk
    Fills my senses

              Red berries
                  in the snow
              You and I

Your hair brushes
 Against my arm
I have no breath left

At two o'clock
    Even the moon has gone to bed
I can't sleep when I know
    You are reading my poems

                    A single dark curly hair
                        Stuck to the soap
                    Is all that she left behind

        Rice again...
            You walk in the room and sit
        Down across the table from me
            How delicious the rice

31

Each spring I sang to the cherry blossoms
    One morning you were there
The cherry blossoms sang to me

        It's dark and wintery outside
            The potato man offers his sweet
        Baked yams for sale
        But I have you

        I must sail to Osaka on business
            A clamp tightens
        Around my heart as you wave goodbye
            Why didn't I learn this lesson last time?

The lady next door wants me to stop
    Playing the flute so late at night
She doesn't know what it feels like
    When you're not here

                    Locusts take seven years to mature
                      Into adults
                    It has taken me forty-two years
                      And you

A million years
    It took to make this smoothly
Rounded pebble,
    And I'm troubled by having to
Wait till midnight?

The sandal maker is eighty years old
    Each time I visit he points
Out the chair where his wife used to sit
    I nod, understanding

              A graceful crane
                Flies across
            The side of my teacup
              I touch your leg

Which is more pleasurable,
    The bowl or the tea?
The dimple in her cheek as she asks

I thought I might catch another glimpse of you
    Amongst these misty cool bamboo trees
Even though it was so many years ago

                    You say I'm a fool for returning
                        Night after night to the tavern
                    Drinking sake and waiting for
                        Another glimpse of her
                    But I don't know the value
                        Of time

    If I pull the weeds
        And wash the dishes and fix
    The leaks
        When will I have time to see you?

Arms and legs entwined
  Fighting and loving
Much the same

Candle melted
  Bed sheets a wonderful mess
The imprint of your head on my pillow

The blackness of the winter night
    Creeps up the fringes of my silk robe,
No promises were made...
    And none were kept

                You have left my bed
                  Without a word,
                The warm glow of autumn
                  Cools quickly
                With the breath of winter

The vastness inside
    From love's sweet caress
Rivals the velvet jeweled night

The brown thrush
    Chirps greetings to the dawn
Oblivious to the pain
    Of your fleeting touch

                    Brightly colored kites
                        Bob and dance in April's lusty winds
                    I cannot hide
                        My devotion to you

                    I drank plum wine tonight...
                        To forget
                    But with each sweet sip
                        I was reminded of you

梅酒

The dark air is thick
    With memories of last night
The ground is cold beneath my bare feet

           The moon bright in the window
              The sheets are snow covered mountains
           Your hair black as pitch

      The four-armed deity has left us
        Sleep plays in our eyes
      I drink in the stillness of the night

月

光

Spring comes
      In my room
When you awaken

Footsteps
   In the snow
Yet I sleep alone

               Sweet oranges
                  Fill me
               With another hunger

Tomorrow we'll be together
    You will climb the mountain
In my bed

If I know you are spying while I eat
    I put down the sticks
Use my hands and lick my fingers

I hear the sliding
Of the rice paper door
I couldn't have waited any longer

The koi swim silently
As I wait
For my Beloved

Itsu? Itsu? Itsu? (When? When? When?)
Ima! Ima! Ima! (Now! Now! Now!)
Doko? Doko? Doko? (Where? Where? Where?)
Koko! Koko! Koko! (Here! Here! Here!)

It's snowing in Kyoto
The next train
Takes me back to you

                    You were etched into my mind
                    With warm sake
                    And the drizzling Kyoto sky

    O-cha
        Honorable tea
    Oh Hiro

I hang my yukata
  And turn
To you

                    A square sheet of paper
                      Golden designs
                    Remembering him as I crease
                      Each fold

    She screams and writhes
        On the tatami mat
    Not caring who hears
        The old woman next door is crazy

Pussy willows
In a bamboo vase
The scent of you lingers still

She covers her mouth
Embarrassed
Thinking of him

Beneath this silk kimono
I am naked
Why are you not here?

Obasan—
Old Woman—
Take my hand
You know the territory

The persimmon is orange
And sweet
You are pale

I sweep the genkan
And straighten the shoes
The sun rises

He is so bold
 He places a giant daikon
On the tokonama

    The spring rains
     Soften winter's edge
    Your kiss smooths
     My furrowed brow

My husband has
 Gone crazy
He writes poetry all night
 Even with his fingertips
Across my back

Why be a lone monument
　　To yourself
My love?

　　　　　　　In the light of the
　　　　　　　　Lantern
　　　　　　A silhouette passes
　　　　　　　　Her breath quickens

　　　There is no need
　　　　For religion
　　Beyond duty to my master

He met death
    As a falling blossom
Without hesitation
    Or regret

                Open your eyes
                    And you will see
                The master bows deeply
                    With perfection

Woman samurai—
    Put down your iron war fan
And rest here

The monk sits impassively
    Thinking of the essential
Food, prayer and her

              These words
                  Are nothing
              Lay by my side

          Long ago I forced myself
              To forget your name
          But I cannot forget
              Your touch

Waiting has its rewards
   Today I watched
A purple hyacinth
   Exploding

         With a turn
           She moves her fan slightly
       And glances at no one
         In particular

    The blood stained futon
      Like the red cranes
  Of her marriage kimono

The path crosses the courtyard
    You sit in silence—
Watching
    As I step from one stone
To the next

Cloud cover thick,
    Rain trickling
Down frosty panes.
    Reminds me
There are tears on my face.

                        Cat jumps up
                            I put her down.
                        Just another day
                            Without him—
                        Not too hot... not too cold.

    These days,
        Even warm
    Breezy hints of spring
        Can't thaw this heart
    Grown cold with waiting.

Summer sunshine
   Torches my skin and kindles
A flame—
   The memory
Of loves long past.

                  Long slender
                     Willow branches
                  Bend deeply so,
                     In sorrow of
                  His going.

        Wilting, reddish
           Dying carnations.
        Even the flowers
           Have forgotten
        His promise.

Steaming water.
    Rinsed bowl.
Waiting whisk.
    Bright green tea.
Oh, where has the guest gone?

My clever cat,
    Sly creature that she is.
No end to her patience
    But she only waits
For a mouse.

Low hum of conversation
    Then... silence
The curtain open
    And you are gone...

                Like the reflection of starlight
                    Winking in my bucket
                Suddenly
                    The distance between us
                Means nothing

        Pale birches whisper
            Did you come this way?
        They're not telling

你來麼？

No blossom scented breeze
    Ever blew so sweetly
As your sleeping breath
    On my cheek

Pain trickling down
   My finger traces each drop
Laugh lines in your face

            The hand is a simple tool
               But used properly
            It evokes a thousand sighs

Only in my dreams
    Do you lay beside me
How I dread the sunrise

The gate / unlocked
    The door / ajar
My heart / quickens
    Waiting / for darkness
A visit

              Can the willow
                  Resist bending
           To the wind?
                  Will you return soon?

      Heat rises
          To blushing cheeks
      Breath quickens
          In short gasps
      My love has arrived

As a new fallen snow
    Is unmarred and pure
As a spring bud
    Is ready to blossom
The young beauty awaits her prince

                    Sleeping alone last night
                      How to explain
                  The condition
                    Of my bed
                  This morning?

The peacock's cry pierces the calm
    His tail spreads a gaudy display
I turn and catch
    Your smile

                In your dark eyes
                  Half closed
                The moon's reflection
                    Can still be glimpsed

        A storm is coming
           Lightning splits the night
        But you are here
           Already

雷

電

In the night, the rain falls.
   In the morning,
You are gone.

            My small house
               Is empty now;
            Where is my friend?

      The last night in August,
         The moon was full;
      I remember only
         The color of your eyes.

満月

Your cool hand
　　Like silk
Caressing my brow.
　　In this moment at least
I yearn for nothing else.

The ancient pine
    Struck by lightning,
I stole from your bed
    Too soon

As the sun rose
    A thick flock of cranes
Flew away from the island
    Years pass
The loud cries of desire
    Settle into the minds of the young

        The bamboo flute
           Wore out when he played
        One note endlessly

    I thought you were the pearl
        Not the oyster
    Would I have eaten so quickly
        If I knew I could not wear you
    For a lifetime?

Sip hot tea
    As it is served
The pot takes time
    To boil again

                Walls of stone
                    Destroyed by floods
                Sorrow's fortress
                    Ruined by new day's sun

        The old crane
            Walks awkward steps
        But will always know
            How to fly

完